A HIDDEN CAUSE *of* WIDESPREAD HOMELESSNESS

A HIDDEN CAUSE *of* WIDESPREAD HOMELESSNESS

The Innovation-Ingenuity Gap

VICTOR M. ERLICH, PHD, MD

PALMETTO
PUBLISHING
Charleston, SC
www.PalmettoPublishing.com

Copyright © 2024 by Victor M. Erlich, PhD, MD

All rights reserved.

No portion of this book may be reproduced, stored in a retrieval system, or transmitted in any form by any means—electronic, mechanical, photocopy, recording, or other—except for brief quotations in printed reviews, without prior permission of the author.

Hardcover ISBN: 9798822960114
Paperback ISBN: 9798822960121
eBook ISBN: 9798822960138

Table of Contents

I	Marxist Doomsday	1
II	Homelessness in the Innovation-Ingenuity Gap	11
III	Malthus' Failed Prediction	15
IV	FDR's WPA Innovated	18
V	A Modest Proposal	21
VI	If Worse Comes	23
VII	What Other Fantasies Might Neo-Luddites Embrace?	29
VIII	The Breaking News is Even Worse	32
IX	Worse Still	36
X	Inflation and the I-I Gap	40
XI	The I-I Gap and The Magna Carta's Failure	44
XII	Homelessness is Now an International Plague	59
XIII	How Might a Treasured Homeland Be Recreated?	75

1:
Marxist Doomsday

The superior power of population cannot be checked without producing misery or vice.
—Thomas Malthus, Essay on the Principle of Population, 1798

The production of too many useful things results in too many useless people.
—Karl Marx, Economic and Philosophic Manuscripts, 1844

Jude went out, and, feeling more than ever his existence to be an undemanded one, he lay on his back on a heap of litter near the pigsty.
—Thomas Hardy, Jude the Obscure, 1895

In the *Communist Manifesto*, Karl Marx marveled that capitalism "has accomplished wonders far surpassing Egyptian pyramids, Roman aqueducts, and Gothic cathedrals." Almost miraculously, railroads and machine-woven silk stockings suddenly appeared. But Marx considered that a mere prelude to what he had demonstrated in *Das Kapital*: Capitalism inevitably destroys itself.

To support of this apocalyptic assertion, Marx offered two heretofore unrecognized consequences of capitalism. The first was the fatal competition that occurs between companies manufacturing products using the same, static technologies. In this scenario, corporations must compete by lowering prices, which requires a compensatory, stepwise decrease in wages as competition intensifies. Eventually, desperate workers quit because they no longer earn enough to feed their families.

Marx's second type of capitalist self-immolation involved the damage done to the working class in economies where technologies kept innovating. Marx foresaw that corporations would assume ownership of all inventions as they emerged, and since new and improved products often cost more to manufacture and more to buy, only the affluent could afford to thrive, again leaving workers unable to support their families and thus unwilling to work in an economic system where the cost of living inevitably grows faster than wages.

Marx argued that *all* capitalist enterprises would inevitably fail, whatever their operating principles might be. They were all doomed by the absolute need to propel wages into a downward spiral to cover the increasing expenses of progressively complex enterprises.

Our current supermarket, for example, is more productive because innovative technology allows the cashier to register sales more quickly and the stock boy to manage inventory more efficiently; but the value-added goes exclusively to the corporations that own the computers. Fewer employees are needed, and those who continue working are offered minimally improved wages, simply because low-skilled workers inevitably play a diminishing role in a corporation's profitability.

And if corporate executives decide that human cashiers cost too much, they adopt the new technology of customer-operated check-out machines, thus further reducing the need for low-skilled cashiers, whose wages stagnate or even decrease.

But some resourceful cashiers may realize that better jobs have now become available in businesses that design, build, and service these clever checkout machines. Though most of the workers who operated the now-obsolete cash registers would be terminated, those who possessed the skills to thrive in a constantly innovating economy might advance to more creative and better-paying jobs.

Corporations fail, not because their underpaid workers quit working, but because unimaginative CEO's lose the race to manufacture, market, and service the best innovations, which constantly improve. Studebaker ceased to manufacture cars and TWA went out of the airline business, but other automakers and other airlines continued their ever-expanding businesses based on their superlative innovations. Of course, advertisement can help, but hucksterism is no substitute for becoming a gold-medalist in the race to produce a more innovative Boeing, Tesla, or bazooka.

And this race has often benefitted skilled workers. During the las three centuries, innovative capitalism has often provided workers upgraded jobs at better pay. When transportation by horse and buggy no longer provided jobs for wainwrights, buggy-whip makers, and owners of livery stables, the emerging automobile industry offered better-paying jobs on the assembly line, even if those jobs were less satisfying than crafting a buggy whip with your own hands. And when robots commandeered the assembly line, new opportunities arose for those who could design and repair robots, but not for those who couldn't.

In the Twentieth century most workers found ways to master new skills and move up a notch on the economic ladder. Yet it has become increasingly clear that not all workers are able to acquire the necessary skills to keep up with innovation. Capitalists might filch from the proletariat the entire pie of innovation's added value at any given moment, but capitalists may not be the workers' worst problem. Some of those who desperately seek remunerative and meaningful work simply lack the ingenuity to master the necessary skills to obtain well-paying employment in the newly innovated fields of computer-driven robots, even when the capitalists are eager to pay satisfying wages to those who *do* possess the necessary skills.

Though capitalism now provides better jobs for workers who once assembled four-horse carriages, the increasingly complicated skills required by our innovative economy forces many bewildered jobseekers to abandon the pursuit of satisfying employment. Eager to work, they are unable acquire the skills that are required in today's computerized industries. So, they scramble for the many low-paying jobs that are advertised everywhere but pay too little to purchase a home anywhere.

As our Industrial Age advances, corporate innovation steadily outpaces a typical individual's capacity to enhance his or her ingenuity, as demonstrated by Adam Smith in his *Wealth of Nations*, published in the propitious year of 1776. Up to that time, an ingenious blacksmith could make just a few nails a day, while an innovative industrialist could acquire the new machines that rapidly fabricated nails by the thousands. When the blacksmith who had long provided hand-made nails to his grateful community found himself no longer thriving in the new world of mass-production, he had to acquire new skills to design, manufacture, and repair those nail-making machines.

And then he had to learn how to operate the new, massive machines that produced reliable train wheels, as well as the perfectly engineered tracks on which they rolled. It is now clear that many former blacksmiths lack the ingenuity to master any of these new skills, and so they dwindle into poverty, despair, and resentment.

So, in the early Nineteenth century, England's increasingly complex industries provoked a counter revolution. Many resentful workers destroyed the machines that had replaced them. Their hero was Ned Ludd, a mythical figure who dwelt in Sherwood Forest, the old haunt of Robin Hood and his merry men.

Few or none of our currently obsolete laborers recall King Ludd and his angry soldiers, but they unwittingly follow their example as they march under new banners, like the Proud Boys, whose mob-like antics differ little from the Luddite riots of yesteryear. Thus, for two centuries, insufficiently skilled workers have been struggling under the baton of innovative capitalists, who continue to replace them with efficient, non-complaining machines.

Curiously, the fear of being replaced has now spawned Far-Right hoodlums, who chant, "You Will Not Replace Us," without bothering to specify why any sane soul would want to usurp their role as desperate failures. Nevertheless, Antifa, the Proud Boys, and other Ludd-like agitators march against today's malignant capitalists, who pay insufficient wages and taxes, or none at all.

And many of our currently unneeded workers join antisemitic rallies, for many of these believe that the evils of greedy capitalists and greedy Jews are one and the same. After all, Henry Ford, a capitalist himself, warned the world in his four-volume Treatise of 1920 that "The International Jew" would become "The World's Foremost Problem."

Ford, whom we will meet again in a more positive context, had his best-seller translated into many languages, thus providing the foundation of today's antisemitic anger of those who defiantly resist being replaced not only by machine-owning capitalists but specifically by the greedy Jews, who have again become scapegoats for piggish capitalists.

And since constantly improving innovation assures that progress moves forward at a faster and faster pace, many workers will find their prospects for meaningful employment constantly shrinking. An old-fashioned mechanic, who once earned a good living in his highly recommended car-repair shop, has now been replaced by a new-age mechanic who works for a convenient Center of Excellence. When this modern mechanic opens the hood, he or she knows exactly what to do with the interrelated computers that have replaced easily recognized sparkplugs and their connections. Those who have mastered the skills to service computer-driven automobiles thrive, but those who lack these advanced skills find themselves resentfully unemployable.

Marx was wrong about capitalism destroying itself via competition between corporations that used either static or innovative technology, but there exists a third problem with capitalism that Marx did not anticipate. We are now living in an age when innovative capitalists, without malice, winnow out those who lack necessary skills from those who *do* possess the wherewithal to perform the increasingly complex work that makes life meaningful and remunerative, a process that should please nobody, not even the winners, who must dwell amongst angry losers.

Some of these "undemanded" workers (Thomas Hardy's word) may be poorly educated, burdened by mental illness, or addicted to drugs and alcohol, but currently many potential workers, who previously thrived without ever suffering from addiction or mental illness, are finding themselves unable to keep up with the demand for workers with advanced skills. And so they are easily tempted to join those who have already found succor in drugs and booze, which quickly render a potential worker even less prepared for a self-supporting life. This is so not because of the high cost of housing, but because the homeless cannot keep up with the rapid pace of innovation. Over time, innovation naturally outpaces the improvement of individual ingenuity by ever-increasing margins, with few realizing the scale of the slowly accumulating damages.

If this is an important cause of our current homelessness, then we have imagined an incorrect chain of causality to explain our mushrooming encampments (See Judea Pearl's *Book of Why* for a discussion of the difficulties encountered when trying to determine causality). Our current thinking about the cause of homelessness goes something like this: mental disease and addiction, coupled with racism, inequity, and unfair exclusion from well-paying jobs have forced increasing numbers of oppressed people to seek shelter wherever they can. And thus any attempt to evict them from their last attempt to survive is cruel punishment for merely trying to live.

Those who take this exculpatory approach to unhealthy and dangerous encampments are now going to court to compel our humane cities to recognize that evicting campers is unconstitutional. According to Kate Walters, a reporter for KUOW in Seattle, Judge David Keenan ruled correctly that the City Council of Seattle violated the US Constitution when it ordered the removal of an encampment from Woodland Park on 5/10/2022.

Megan Farmer, a photographer for KUOW News in Seattle, captured the huge crane that swept up the tents, garbage, and bicycles that sprawled beneath a large sign that proclaimed the principles that governed the encampment: HOUSING FOR ALL! SERVICES NOT SWEEPS!

Ms. Framer's photo shows that the campers in Woodland Park are *not* obstructing access to Woodland Park, *not even* for a large crane and its enormous yellow mandible. But it is also obvious that parents would consider this campsite a danger to their children's safety as they scampered about in this green space adjacent to the Woodland Park Zoo.

But according to Ms. Kate Walter's, this worry did not concern Judge Keenan:

> The ruling from judge David Keenan found that one of the city's frequently used reasons for clearing encampments is overly broad in its definition and, in some cases, unconstitutional. At issue in this case is the city's removal labeled as "Obstruction." For such camps, city rules do not require prior notice, outreach, storage of belongings, or offers of shelter, aspects required for other removals. Keenan's ruling acknowledges that there are instances when the City has the right to remove camps without notice, for instance if there's and immediate safety risk, or a true obstruction of a public sidewalk. But the ruling also states that the city defines "obstruction" too broadly, making some removals unconstitutional.

"Under the obstruction definition, the City can remove a tent or person anywhere in a park, and anywhere on a public sidewalk, irrespective of actual obstruction … if there is a safety risk." But even an "immediate safety risk," Keenan wrote, renders orders to remove entire tent encampments cruel punishment [under the Eighth Amendment] to the extent that they rely on the overbroad "Obstruction" definition, because that definition "allows the City to move unhoused people without offering them shelter."

A neighbor whose children often played in Woodland Park would quickly note judge Keenan's problematic thinking. He acknowledges that campers can be legally removed if they present either an "immediate safety risk" or a "true obstruction." Thus an encampment that *does* present an "immediate safety risk" is sufficient justification for removal even it is not obstructing sidewalks. But, says the ACLU, even though many campers do present a danger, they cannot be removed if the city refuses to honor its obligation to house them elsewhere.

One might think that the proven prevalence in encampments of mental disease, drugs, drunkenness, and violence would constitute a sufficient threat to the safety of children to override a city's invented obligation to house drunkards before they protect children. But The American Civil Liberties Union of Washington State believed that evicting campers was unconstitutional, and so in 2019 their lawyers made this argument in court:

> Unhoused people have a right of privacy in the places that they call home. Absent a significant governmental interest and an offer of shelter, the City cannot simply invade the homes of people.

Judge Keenan agreed with the ACLU that the City of Seattle had no "significant governmental interest" in the safety of children, and therefore ACLU's assessment of the homeless encampment in Woodland Park was correct, for the encampment contains nothing but "the homes of people" who "have a right of privacy." And this right is paramount, requiring no concern about the prevalence of disease and violence in these sacrosanct "homes" of homeless people.

The questionable reasoning of the good Judge Keenan is worth comparing with actual crime statistics in Burien, a city just 14 miles from the Woodland Park Zoo. On 9/16/2023, *The Burien News* reported increasing crime in the city's encampments:

> King County Sheriff's Department has compiled crime numbers for the homeless encampments in Burien since January 2023. The number shows a clear uptick in illegal activity and demand on police services wherever an encampment is set up. … The data shows a large surge in crime. [And even worse], those who have seen trafficking and child rape, possession of stolen goods in shopping carts, and open drug selling, [say that] these numbers seem understated. Business owners and managers in the area have told the city council that they report only one in ten crimes due to lack of protection [presumably for the complaining neighbors and shop-owners] and the time required to fill out paperwork.

Seattle's City Attorney has appealed Judge Keenan's ruling, but for now it stands, thus raising the question of why the honorable judge is so supportive of campers who unpredictably might engage in "trafficking and child rape." But before we address our culture's new tolerance for malicious vagrancy, let us consider the epidemiology of the homeless problem.

11:
Homelessness in the Innovation-Ingenuity Gap

As we review the epidemiology of homelessness, let us keep in mind that despite the fact that twenty-five years ago the prevalence of alcoholism, mental illness, and disabling AIDS was not much lower than now, the prevalence of homelessness is currently skyrocketing. Yes, the homeless population has a high prevalence of mental disease, disability, and substance abuse, but it is unlikely that these medical problems cause the majority of homelessness. More likely, much of homelessness is the result of the silent process that allows individual ingenuity to lag further and further behind corporate innovation. Even if a society's capacity for innovation advances only a tad faster than an individual's capacity to adapt, the difference will eventually cause unsurmountable difficulties for those who falter as they struggle to keep up.

Early in Seattle's history, a few homeless drunks camped along Yesler Way, where sober citizens wouldn't live, because dangerous logs were skidded down from Seattle's forested hills to its port. But over decades unsanitary encampments have sprung up throughout Seattle. And "Skid Roads" (or "Rows," as they were called during my childhood in Los Angeles) have metastasized all over the country, from New York's East River to the beachfront of Venice, California, from sea to shining sea, where hypodermic needles sparkle in the sun.

Who are these unfortunate souls? A report from the Centers for Disease Control and Prevention, published on March 2, 2017, gives us some idea:

> On any given night, hundreds of thousands of people are homeless in the United States.... Homelessness is closely connected to declines in physical and mental health; homeless persons experience high rates of health problems such as HIV infection, alcohol and drug abuse, mental illness, tuberculosis, and other conditions.

To substantiate these claims, the CDC draws on studies such as "The Epidemiology of the Homeless Population and Its Impact on an Urban Emergency Department" by Dr. Jason D'Amore, *et al.*, published in *Academic Emergency Medicine* in November 2001:

> In the United States, the homeless population is estimated to be between 4 and 13.5 million persons, and 7.5% of the general population will become homeless at sometime in their lifetimes.

The authors then use data from one urban hospital to compare a group of 252 homeless patients in the ER with a control group of 88 patients in the same ER during the same period who enjoyed a fixed domicile. Rates of various diseases are presented in the form of rates in the homeless group versus the rates in the domiciled group (the homeless percentages are shown in **bold**):

> History of HIV infection **35%** vs. 13%; history of tuberculosis **49%** vs. 15%; history of depression **70%** vs. 15%; history of schizophrenia **27%** vs.7%, history of alcoholism **81%** vs. 15%.

In 2001, the homeless group was obviously burdened by more disease than the domiciled group, and these numbers are likely worse now. For, in our day, when the homeless have access to drugs like fentanyl that are more toxic than the booze favored by the bums and hobos of yesteryear, it is likely that our park-campers carry more disabling infectious diseases, such as inadequately treated HIV and refractory tuberculosis.

During the two decades that have elapsed since these Emergency-Room statistics were compiled, relentless innovation has marched on. Low-skilled jobs on the ranch and in lumbar camps have vanished, and thus many low-skilled workers have fewer opportunities to get paid for hard work, earn respect, and happily put down their tools when the dinner bell rings.

Also long gone are the barely satisfying jobs as a hotel bellhop, a porter in a railroad station, or a muscular coalminer. Even hale and hardy laborers now find their skills unneeded as innovation replaces little human engines with mammoth machines that finish everything faster and cheaper than Paul Bunyan. And so, this continuously enlarging group of former lumberjacks and coal miners has become progressively forlorn, having been forced to dwell adjacent to, or actually in, Jude-the-Obscure's pigsty, now called a homeless encampment, from which only those with better skills can escape.

If it is indeed true that the current pace of innovation forces an increasing number of our under-skilled citizens into toxic encampments, then we should give this worsening problem a name and propose a pertinent solution. Simply decrying the price of housing, the paucity of mental-health services, and the piggishness of capitalism will not suffice. Nor will the American habit of throwing money at inadequately understood problems be of any practical use.

Perhaps we might profitably focus our attention on our "increasing ingenuity-innovation gap." Or, since we now lived in a soup of acronyms, such as GDP and IRS, perhaps we would be wise to study our increasing I-I Gap, that growing distinction between those who possess sufficient ingenuity to participate in our constantly innovating economy, and those who don't.

Picture, say, twenty high-school students who are set against each other in a 50-yard dash. The fastest of them do not finish very far in front of the slowest. But in a 100-yard race, the winner finishes farther ahead of the stragglers. After a quarter-mile race, the separation between the fast and the slow is even greater, and after a mile race, there are some runners who are so winded that they cannot cross the finish line. And after a 5-mile race, we find an even larger gap between the swift and the slow.

The longer a race goes on, the clearer it becomes that some are faster than others, and many are not fit to race at all, some because of bad behavior like smoking and drug addiction, and some for problems that are nobody's fault, such as asthma. But the asthmatic runner might still become a neurosurgeon (I am acquainted with one), while the despondent addict in an encampment is doomed to remain useless, unless we deal with the homeless problem as it is: the longer the Industrial Revolution goes on, the larger grows the population in the I-I gap, and thus our misery increases, especially in our tumultuous urban centers.

III:
Malthus' Failed Prediction

The race to improve ones ingenuity fast enough to keep up with our rapidly innovating society has gone on since the Industrial Revolution in the Eighteenth century, to the point that we have now accumulated an overwhelming number of stragglers.

It would not be wise to cancel the race, for that would deprive us of the necessary innovation to feed, educate, and culturally enrich our expanding population, with eight billion souls currently aboard this hurtling planet. For our ongoing innovation, with its growing demand on individual ingenuity, is exactly what has prevented the disaster predicted in 1798 by Thomas Malthus. His *Essay on the Principle of Population* entirely ignores the dynamics of human innovation and ingenuity, the former reliably outrunning the latter.

Instead, Malthus blamed the entire risk to humanity's well-being on arithmetic laws. Population, says Malthus, will grow exponentially, but food production will grow linearly, eventually causing fatal starvation for all. But this did not turn out to be a problem. The world's population is now better fed than it was in Malthus's day, and in many nations many are obese.

Our urgent but yet unrecognized problem is that innovation outpaces the capacity of many stragglers to maintain self-sufficiency.

We have produced an unintended competition that yields winners and losers of a type that neither Marx nor Malthus foresaw. For increasing numbers of our fellow citizens, individual ingenuity lags further and further behind corporate innovation, marooning the stragglers in one kind of pigsty or another.

So what are we to do? What kind of innovation might solve this worsening dilemma? We can put losing racehorses out to pasture, but we cannot do that to human stragglers; advances in our ethics over the millennia have made this unthinkable. But unthinkable or not, we have put many of our brethren out to pasture in city parks and under freeways.

Perhaps we should apply our capacity to innovate to the very problem that our superlative innovation has created. The challenge is to provide capitalism's benefits for all without killing capitalism itself, which is the only goose known to lay the majority of mankind's golden eggs.

Of course a practical solution has not yet been developed, but it is the very nature of human innovation to solve the riddles of how to square the circle and bring light into darkness. Geometers showed how the square-area of a circle could be calculated by the clever formula of multiplying the irrational number pi by the circle's radius squared; and we invented the candle so Abraham Lincoln could read Euclid in the dark, then the light bulb, then the computer screen. We are not condemned to remain in darkness of any kind, nor must we groan forever as we look down from our innovated heights on fellow citizens as they molder in homeless filth.

What might an innovative solution be to the problems of those who trail behind the needs and demands of an innovative world? Food stamps for those in tents will not likely improve the campers' ingenuity beyond resorting to the clever trick of trading food for alcohol. Nor will a universal basic income be of much help for those campers who would likely use the funds for a better tent and better drugs. And how will we handle those who insist on their right to defecate on the sidewalks of San Francisco while allowing their personal ingenuity to lay fallow in Golden Gate Park?

Whatever solution we adopt, we might do well to consider the ethical approach to the emerging viral pandemics, as laid out recently by E.J. Emanuel in the *New England Journal of Medicine* of 5/21/2020. And we'll have to pay the bill, using funds drawn from the current wasteful spending by states and municipalities on the poorly understood cause of homelessness. We may even need to raise taxes.

Let us assume that at the onset we will find nothing to uplift some of our stragglers, but if we can help many, we might apply further innovations to those who were not served by our initial efforts.

IV:
FDR's WPA Innovated

There are even now innovative solutions to the problem of homelessness, some of which are at least partially successful and resemble what I will now propose (See, for example, *LifeMoves* in Mountain View, California). I am thinking of a campus built in the manner of a college dormitory complex, but richer in services. Perhaps there would be three or four dorm-like buildings surrounding a central quad, which would include a cafeteria, stores, trade-shops, studios, classrooms, and green spaces. Instead of single rooms, the dorms would feature small studio apartments, and some larger spaces for families. Prepared food would be inexpensively available in the central cafeteria, which will need employees drawn from those residents who wish training in hospitality services.

Other residents in our college-like campuses may wish to work in the quad's grocery store, earning a stipend as they train for entry-level jobs as a steppingstone toward better jobs in our constantly innovating world. Shops on our hypothetical campuses could train those who hoped to become carpenters, electricians, plumbers. Other shops could train artisans how to create and market hand-made goods, say, well-knit Irish sweaters, glass-blown chandeliers, and expertly crafted chef knives.

Training to become a plasterer in the old-fashioned Italian style might attract a former expert in pitching tents, as this skill is still in demand. Some of those who were helped to forgo drugs and alcohol in a campus rehabilitation center may wish to be trained as drug counselors, able to serve in the neighborhoods where they once lived safely, until they themselves became addicted. And a few newly motivated strivers might learn how to repair the robots that are now usurping work from those who were once handy with wrenches.

For those who dropped out of high school, courses in obtaining a GED can be offered. More advanced studies can be offered as residents liberate their intelligence from the ravages of intoxicants. Well-designed green spaces and athletic fields can offer not only exercise but also training for those who might become tennis- or golf-instructors. For, some human needs can be satisfied with ideas that do not require the innovation of fancy gadgets.

Since it would be foolish to set up such mini-centers in the heart of large and expensive cities, one might choose less-expensive locations within easy transportation to a big city, perhaps a place on a lake, where a former camper can learn how to sail and how to earn a living by teaching others the art of sailing. These imaginary villages, of course, would not be anything like our current counterproductive shelters, and thus they might persuade some of our obstinate campers to forsake government-sponsored drug-injection centers, which are nothing but dead ends.

Taxpayers who support these new opportunities would soon learn whether their taxes were now being better spent on innovative villages than on wasteful programs for the stubborn problem of homelessness. In Seattle, the City Council's 2020 budget included more than $100 million for the homeless, for which impatient taxpayers have received an increase of toxic encampments. In some quarters of Seattle, these campers have forced many businesses to close because of pillage and violence.

Those expensive tents nestled in parks are usually shoplifted from large sporting-equipment stores whose employees are too intimidated by the looters to call the police, who are too overwhelmed to respond to "petty crimes." In San Francisco, theft is ignored unless the loot is worth more than $950.00, with each of multiple heists on the same day considered individually, thus limiting a thief's daily haul to whatever multiple of $950.00 can be acquired before Cinderella's clock strikes midnight.

It is not a fairy tale to imagine an innovative society where most of its citizens can find life-enhancing work. And, as is well-known in the world of business, every economic success has a cascading benefit, as it increases the money supply. With their skillset improved, many former campers would now earn and spend money, and the tax-paying shopkeepers who made this possible would profit from new, paying customers, with the number of looters manageably reduced.

V :
A Modest Proposal

Taxpayers often complain that our expensive social programs do not undergo a sufficient accounting. The following is offered only as a rough version of how we might assess the worth of our efforts to solve the problem of the inevitably increasing gap between entrepreneurial innovation and insufficient ingenuity. Taxpayers demand and deserve better programs of accounting than those now reported on television regarding new programs that reliably fail.

The programs I have just offered treat our national problem as if it were a single entity, though a proper accounting should be done for each of the many encampments that spring up under a wide variety of local conditions. Since we have known since the time of the Greek philosopher Heraclitus that everything changes all the time, the following is naught but a plausible way of estimating the state of our progress.

Taking the U.S. as a whole, there are about 8 million potential workers among an estimated total 10 -13 million homeless campers (the others are children, the disabled, and the elderly, who require separate approaches). The term "potential" assumes that with innovative treatment a gratifying number of drunks, addicts, and school-dropouts can be rehabilitated.

Let us then take the current estimate of full-time employees in the US as about 120 million, and the current estimate of unfilled jobs as about 9 million (the official estimation is about 8 million, but many jobs are not advertised because the prospect of finding a qualified candidate is too low to justify the expense).

The US Department of Housing and Urban Development estimates that in both 2016 and 2017 the rate of growth of homelessness was 9%. But since we are assuming that individual ingenuity lags further and further behind innovation, let us estimate that homelessness is now growing at about 10% annually.

With an innovative effort, and a determination to track results, we may be able to improve our civic life at a price well worth paying.

VI:
If Worse Comes

If it is indeed true that the rate of growth of individual ingenuity is significantly slower than the rate of growth of entrepreneurial innovation, then the gap between the two will inevitably continue to grow, thus creating an increasing number of people who are unable to adapt. And since the general level of education in the USA keeps falling, what will happen when our best efforts to solve the homeless problem succumb to the brute reality of unassailable numbers?

Of course, it is possible that the problem of homelessness *is indeed* insoluble but accepting that possibility as fact will likely spawn missed opportunities. Malthus and Marx mistakenly believed that they had numbers to prove that capitalism was doomed, even though it wasn't. So we should avoid concluding that we have the numbers to prove that capitalism is doomed by dawdling ingenuity's tendency to fall further and further behind galloping innovation.

Since this nefarious progression is certain to worsen if not treated, how might our current crisis evolve if current trends persist? Might we find ourselves living in a society where homelessness is only a small part of our social malaise? The failure of a growing number of our citizens to find rewarding employment will likely lead to more anger and more violence. Cities that were once peaceful might suffer repetitive bouts of mayhem, as was the case during Portland's 100 nights of rioting in the summer of 2020.

In our new dystopia, we may find homeless encampments near schoolyards, causing further damage to our faltering system of education. Bullets that ricochet here and there kill innocent bystanders, including children, and police officers will stand back because they are despised for what they do and what they do not do. Some of those who still value our civilization will fear to venture out to our theaters and world-class museums but stay at home with loaded guns, terrified by the angry residents in the pigsty just outside their shuttered windows.

And there is still more to fear. An increasing I-I Gap might prove worse than the individual problems of homelessness, addiction, and random violence. These maladies might easily exacerbate each other, thus producing a yearning for a magical salvation from having failed to find a place in the sun. In these dark shadows, desperate stragglers might become idolatrous worshippers of the sun and the wind, as if those ancient gods, Helios and Zephyrus, could satisfy their idealistic need for inexhaustible clean energy without causing a regrettable collapse of our energy-dependent civilization.

And when these mythical gods inevitably fail, those who are still suffering from insufficient ingenuity might embrace the smiling politicians who serve the gods of "Democratic Socialism" that are more consoling than the chancy powers of human creativity and innovation.

One common feature shared by the various attempts to establish a society based on socialist principles is the difficulty of providing meaningful and remunerative work to everyone who seeks these satisfactions. Marx, himself a creative thinker, hoped to establish an economic system that magically produced a sufficient abundance of material goods to allow those who wished to use leisure to pursue nobler goals. In his 1875 *Critique of the Gotha Programme*, he hallowed a long-held idea in socialist circles:

> In a higher phase of communist society, after the enslaving subordination of the individual to the [capitalist] division of labor ... and all the springs of cooperative [i.e., communist] wealth flow more abundantly—only then can the narrow horizon of bourgeois right be crossed ... and society inscribes on its banners: **From each according to his ability, to each according to his needs!**

Of course, this optimistic worldview quickly degenerated into an abusive class system, where an authoritarian Politburo determined both the ability and the need of every comrade and then assigned him or her to a proper niche, subject to revised orders issued by the wise First Secretary of the Communist Party, whoever that might be.

Since no human being can know from the onset what the best pathway to his or her still-uncertain goal is, it is even less likely that a commissar will place every anonymous comrade in the most advantageous slot. Only an individual's freedom to make mistakes and to change course has any chance of achieving a just and workable end.

But few comrades in Soviet Russia enjoyed the freedom of being at home in the right job, so many became homeless as communes failed, one after another. As one of my patients, an escapee from a Russian commune, explained to me at the University of Washington Medical Center, "They pretended to pay us, and we pretended to work—and the tractors that they sent never arrived—or they arrived without gasoline—nor did the fertilizer arrive during sowing time—so the crops failed."

In the summer of 2004, my son and I bicycled around the "Golden Chain" of old Muscovite Capitol Cities that had been serially destroyed by Mongol conquerors until Tsar Peter the Great put an end this repetitive curse. During this tour we visited an abandoned commune, where we picnicked on a marooned wagon among decaying homes, rusting equipment. and crumbling outbuildings. My son shot this photo:

Prime Minister Gorbachev eventually brought this economic wreckage to a merciful conclusion. But strangely, new Masters of Business Administration in our floundering West have taken upon themselves the self-righteous task of providing work for those who lack sufficient skills to seize one of the new opportunities in our innovative economy. Oblivious and unchallenged, these MBA's have created many unnecessary and even disruptive jobs that that allow many of our new administrators the illusion that they are accomplishing something important and fulfilling, much like the make-work commissars of the Soviet Union.

This busy-body leadership has inevitably led to a widespread discontent in both the providers and the recipients of our newly incompetent services. Many victims of our new regulators and administrators report that the services that they now receive have been significantly degraded.

For example, in the last years of my medical practice, our independent group was acquired by our University Hospital. During our first year under the new regime, we learned that our hospital's medical staff added a single physician and 46 new administrators, who, without any discussion, added several new employees to our office staff, none of whom were needed before we were acquired. The so-called Medical Assistants who had been assigned to our office had hoped to participate in the healing arts, but instead they were kept busy managing to-and-fro messages from patients, other doctors, and administrators, who demanded explanations for many previously non-existent "issues," such as why we couldn't fit in patients after our clinic was closed, and why we were spending so much money on paper, and why so many scheduled patients never showed up in our clinic.

That the administrators themselves initiated and ran our new online appointment system that often scheduled new patients in the wrong clinic at the wrong time was not considered relevant. Nor did our administrators ever ask us why we ran a more efficient and profitable office by having our capable staff answer our phones in person and make appointments, solve problems, and answer questions without enmeshing callers in a tedious phone tree.

Of course, this rendered everybody involved chronically less effective and more dissatisfied, including physicians, medical assistants, and their administrators. The platoons of new medical administrators who ran our practice had no idea about how the ancient calling of medicine was practiced before it was taken over by new officials who left the followers of Hippocrates and Galen virtually homeless, often forcing them into early retirement.

Because older physicians have more-than-adequate savings, they of course do not wind up in homeless encampments, but they do illustrate one of the many ways that hard-working professionals and skilled tradesmen find it increasingly difficult to feel at home in their formerly rational homeland.

Nobody feels at home in land of foolish make-work, but this unexpected disappointment often makes compassionate health providers more tolerant of fellow citizens who are similarly discontent with their current life in tents.

This growing compassion for poor, working-age campers living in squalid encampments is just one of the many surprising phenomena of our new world, where many sympathize with the homeless who daily undermine the safety of those who dwell in the prosperous realm above the I-I Gap. And the activists who entertain the fantasy that supporting mayhem improves the justice of our society are not alone.

VII:
What Other Fantasies Might Neo-Luddites Embrace?

Currently, a number of unanticipated issues plague our social harmony in ways that a mere seventy-five years ago were not even a whisper in anybody's mind. Among these are gender dysphoria and its associated quarrels about the correct use of pronouns and bathrooms, the disparity of outcomes between those who enjoy the benefits of innovative medicine and those who do not, as well as the increasing Income-Gap between those who can pay rent and those who cannot.

Every week, the *New England Journal of Medicine* cites examples of these disparities, which have led to an increasing hatred between earnest souls who have conflicting views of these contentious issues. Much of our current angry squabbling appears to stem directly from the very nature of the I-I Gap.

Let us consider a few of our current, overheated debates. When a sentient human being finds himself or herself unneeded in a thriving economy, he or she quite naturally might wish to be a different somebody. Perhaps one would be more successful if one belonged to another gender, or had closer affinities with Native Americans, or had more tattoos and more piercings, or became an influencer rather than an unsuccessful producer, or a critic of capitalism rather than a contributor to a perverse system that unfairly excludes those with supposedly insufficient ingenuity.

With a better set of qualities to display, one might be more in demand, and thus own an attractive home rather than a stollen tent, and be able to send a child to Harvard University Medical School, where, according to Heather Mac Donald in the Summer 2023 issue of *City Journal*, there are a host of administrators to assure that every medical student will be accorded a sense of acceptance in a diverse community that features inclusivity, equity, and a newly-invented right to enjoy a feeling of *belonging*, which is yet another term recently added to politically-correct speech:

> Among the medical school's twenty-five dedicated diversity professionals are a dean for Diversity and Community Partnership; an assistant dean, Office for Diversity and Community Partnership; a faculty assistant director, Office for Diversity Inclusion and Community Partnership; and a program manager in the Harvard Catalyst Program for Faculty Development and Diversity Inclusion. The medical school and the dental school [also take pride in their] Joint Committee on the Status of Women; and the medical school [also boasts an] Office of Recruitment and Multicultural Affairs.
>
> The Chan School of Public Health's four diversity positions include a chief officer for Diversity, Inclusion, and **Belonging** …

Ms. Mac Donald then notes that Harvard Medical School's constantly expanding diversity programs have persisted for more than twenty years without any significant improvement in their insufficiently diverse faculty and student body. Part of the reason for this dismal failure, says Ms. Mac Donald, likely stems from the difficulty of finding a sufficient number of candidates who can master both the increasingly innovated skills that are necessary to practice the complicated sciences of physiology and medicine, *and* the increasingly prohibitive standards that are required to be a member in good standing at an institution that places its highest value on Diversity, Equity, Inclusivity, and Belonging.

VIII:
The Breaking News is Even Worse

Walter Cronkite, born in 1916, reported on the Nazi bombing of London during WWII, the Allied landing on Normandy Beach, and the Nuremberg trials with a grace and confidence that led to his becoming the anchorman of CBS's Evening News in 1962, where he quickly became "the most trusted man in America." When he signed off every evening by saying, "And that's the way it is," most Americans had no reason to doubt the benevolent man, especially when he was talking about news that really mattered. Whether "Uncle Walter," as he was fondly called by the public, was always letter perfect in his reporting was not as important as the fact that he was always considered trustworthy, which became a standard that American newscasters would continue to respect.

But now, in the age of so-called Fake News, including fake news about fake news, a newscaster cannot even dream of achieving the status of Uncle Walter. After much show-biz palaver about the crisis on the southern border, the contested 2020 election, the debacle in Afghanistan, and worsening inflation, the "way it is" remains unclear to many, blatantly false to some and obviously true to others, depending on varying notions of the truth.

And, when speaking about the homeless problem, politicians deliberately obfuscate their inability to identify its true causes as they demand more money to apply failed solutions to a crisis that has steadily worsened under their overly generous care, especially in our largest cities. Even investigative journalists turn to fabricated scapegoats for an explanation of intractable homelessness. The usual villains include greedy landlords, incompetent mental-health officials, unsympathetic employers who decline to hire potentially excellent employees who need nothing more than a bit of encouragement. The politicians say, and the newscasters obligingly confirm, that they are doing their very best to solve this vexed problem, hindered only by politicians of the other party, whichever that might be.

One might wonder why highly demanded and well-paid newscasters are so eager to support those politicians who propose all sorts of ineffective solutions while doing little to stop Antifa's blockades of highways. Virtuous newscasters will, when necessary, defend the rioters of Portland against Trump's malignant attempt to send federal troops to rescue Portland from more than a hundred nights of rioting. Here is an excerpt from Mayor Ted Wheeler's open letter to President Trump on 8/29/2020, a document enthusiastically endorsed by the media:

> On behalf of the City of Portland: No thanks ... We don't need your politics of division and demagoguery ... Portlanders are onto you. We have already seen your reckless disregard for human life in your bumbling response to the COVID pandemic. And we know you've reached the conclusion that images of violence and vandalism are your only ticket to reelection.

At face value, Wheeler's accusation that Trump wished to send federal troops to Portland only to show accusatory images of "violence and vandalism" was obviously untrue, for these images were already splashed across the front pages of the national press. And the "bumbling response to the COVID pandemic" was not particularly pursued by Trump, who actively supported the rapid development of a semi-effective vaccine, but by the Democratic Governor of New York who had dispatched Covid patients to nursing homes where they infected vulnerable inpatients, many of whom died.

But Wheeler's blustering response to the riots in his city is not my point here. I rather want to understand why he and others who live safely above the I-I Gap are so eager to support the angry campers and their rioting supporters who hate everybody thriving in the mysterious realm above them.

Part of the explanation of why politicians are so tolerant of the ongoing violence in tent encampments derives from the I-I Gap, which actually has an even lower level. Those *in* the I-I Gap struggle to elevate themselves into the Innovative Class, where one can enjoy the rewards of success, while those who lack sufficient preparation to make even the smallest effort to improve their lot are forced to occupy an even lower level of frustration and anger, where they turn to violence and vandalism.

Now it so happens that many of those who have soared high above the I-I Gap find themselves rich and famous for accomplishments that might not be so favorable after they flunk their next audition, lose their next election, or find themselves dismissed from the Nightly News without any justification mentioned. This fear of a comeuppance has apparently motivated some famous actors and talking heads to express sympathy for those in the invisible I-I Gap who struggle to pay their rent and grocery bills, and an even deeper sympathy for the thugs who fester so far below the I-I

Gap that they can manage no more than making life miserable for themselves and those who share their neighborhood.

It is easy to understand why comfortable citizens feel compassion for disabled folks with limited capacities, but many find it almost impossible to grasp why some of those those who thrive in the Innovative Class are so eager to support those seemingly healthy young men who are hellbent on pleasing themselves while destroying themselves and undermining their own civilization.

With little understanding of the consequences of innovation, perhaps the successful intuit that the mysterious universe might randomly fling them from their prosperous realm into the undeserved Hades of Homelessness. And thus they respond with limitless compassion for those compatriots who have inexplicably fallen.

Though I base this hypothesis on mere observation, it would explain why there is so much sympathy for those who are now mired in hostile despondency. For, the plight of others often serves as a fearful omen to those who are already teetering on the cusp of inadequacy.

IX:
Worse Still

If worse does come to worst, how might we rescue ourselves from this pyrrhic dilemma that we have created by allowing human innovation to overwhelm our capacity to keep up with it? What innovation might suffice to cut this Gordian Knot without recourse to the brute force enacted by our recent rioters, and even by Alexander the Great, the first to unknot an emblematically intractable problem with brute force? Because Alexander trusted his experience of conquering the entire world, he approached the famous riddle of untying the cunningly woven Gordian Knot with his famous capacity to apply overwhelming force. So clever Alexander simply slashed the knot open with a single blow of his well-trained sword.

But since this mythic riddle was nothing but a buffoonish challenge to untether Zeus's favorite oxcart, it cannot provide a sound example of solving a difficult problem. For though Alexander did indeed cut the Gordian Knot and thereby earned Great Zeus's support for his conquest of the known world, it did not hinder the Fickle God from offing the hero on his way home.

Worse, Alexander's fellow devotees to Aristotle's civilization likely expected their hero to offer a reasoned solution to the problem of the Gordian Knot (Alexander himself was tutored by Aristotle).

But instead he demonstrated that brute force leads to nothing but death, as was the case in Homeric texts. In his *Iliad*, Homer has prophetic Casandra declare to her vengeful Greek compatriots, "For me waits destruction by the two-edged sword."

Force is indeed sometimes required from the right side of the two-edged sword, says Casandra, but foolish force from the wrong side is treacherous and must be rejected. But of course the indefatigable armies of Agamemnon ignored Casandra and flung a thousand ships at the Trojans to gain nothing but mutual destruction.

So too, the solution to the problem of rescuing innovation's homeless outcasts may not lay in forcing them into treatments that they abhor, nor in using firepower to extinguish the red glare of their riots, but in recognizing the actual cause of sociopathic homelessness. The innovative civilization of the West has found itself unprepared to manage the mayhem that it itself created by allowing galloping innovation to outpace the dawdling progression of personal ingenuity, which abandons a constantly increasing number of stragglers to infuriated uselessness.

If this is so, we must innovate a better approach to our yet insoluble homeless misery, something like that which is suggested in this artful painting of "Alexander Cutting the Gordian Knot" by Fedele Fischetti, a Neapolitan artist of the Eighteen century:

Fischettii coils his version of the snake-like Knot around the oxcart's tongue, setting it at the base of an equilateral triangle. At the triangle's apex sits a monumental but unrecognizable human figure, the apparent overseer of the armed Alexander and his helmeted soldiers, who complete the triangle's sides. At the very center of this composition are shadowy sages who just might have deeper ideas than those of the mighty Alexander with a sharp little sword. The artistry of the painter suggests a more creative, a more balanced, even a Euclidian solution to the knottiest of problems. Inevitably, the solution to the problem of the ever-increasing I-I gap will come in the form of enhanced human creativity.

Perhaps so, but we cannot assume that this murky figure hovering over Fischetti's Gordian Knot is humane in the best sense, and not an overbearing thyrant. In any case, a sea of troubles churns before the supervising eyes of Fischetti's wise man in the sky.

X :
Inflation and the I-I Gap

Occasionally, one might hear somebody's grandfather say something like this:

> Things were not like like this when I was young—I bought my first house for $5,000, and I paid cash—In South Dakota we believed that you shouldn't be buying anything with somebody else's money—And, besides that, if you buy on credit, you inflate the cost of housing for everybody else—It's obvious that credit causes inflation—More money in the marketplace creates more *demand* without creating more *supply*.

But inflation creeps up so slowly that few shoppers understand it. If inflation drives the cost of essential goods up 10% yearly for three years, and then the Feds manage to drive it back down to 3% in the fourth year, the ruling political party congratulates itself, and many troubled citizens take a sigh of relief, thinking that prices are now going back to what they used to be.

But simple arithmetic, which is no longer well-taught in our elementary schools, shows that compound interest at 10% yearly

A Hidden Cause of Widespread Homelessness

for three years, then compounded at 3% yearly for one more year, increases a weekly grocery bill of $100 four years earlier to about $137, which is no relief at all. Food is still expensive and getting more burdsome, even if it is, for the moment, getting worse more slowly. Thus the reduction of inflation from 10% to 3% should be welcomed but not celebrated.

In fact, a run of excessive inflation actually pushes even more citizens into the I-I Gap, where they become more disgruntled and less able to understand the forces that are squeezing them. This can drive a formerly proud truck-driver to become a smash-and-grab burgler, and it can even persuade a once reasonable youngster into the newly-invented wheel of magical fortunes. Once in this fantastical world, our young man might reasonably say, "Other people are doing much better than I, so I will make myself one of them—If I'm a middling athlete on my highschool swim team, perhaps I can be a champion on the U.S. Women's Olympic Team—Mr. Rogers on TV told me I can be anything I want to be—And so I'm a champion Lady Swimmer.

And if I'm a Physician Assistant I can join my fellow PA's who are petitioning my State Legislature to permit Phasician Assistants to practice medicine as fully licensed physicians—In Washington State, a Bill along these lines just barely failed in a recent session of the Legislature. Since hardly anybody can perceive the existence and nature of the I-I Gap, the identity of the culprits who created it must also be unknown.

Thus the distraught victims who feel unfairly imprisoned behind these invisible bars are eager to discover who or what locked them up. It can't be all those illegal immigrants who are falsely accused of charging less than American labor—And it can't be the cheap goods that are manufactured in China, because everybody says that the price of Chinese toasters has nothing to do with the price of tea in San Francisco—And that leaves the usual suspects, either Donald J. Trump, or the conniving Jews of Israel, with whom the former President and his Jewish daugthter are even now committing genocide on the innocent rocketeers of Gaza, at least according to the earnest protesters at our esteemed universities, one of whom, while wearing a burka, holds up a placard demanding that Israel "Cease Genocide," as her academic colleagues display a banner demanding the destruction of Israel "By Any Means Necessary," a euphonism represented by a Palestinian flag placed on the banner's left side in the shape of the entire State of Israel:

Even the US Senator from Vermont placed his impriamatur on this banner by telling the *Guardian* on 1/12/2024 that Biden should "put distance between himself and th Prime Minister Benjamin Netanyahu and the horrific war he is waging against the Palestinian people." Of course the righteous Senator need not mention the horrific war that Hamas is waging against Jews everywhere, because he can see that we live in an age when many are desperate to punish the supposed jailors who keep them locked in the dungeons of the I-I Gap.

None of our current social plagues, including gender confusion, income inequity, medical disparities, and our ever-expanding homelessness, would be overwhelming our current world if it were not for the ever-expanding I-I Gap. Before the I-I Gap became unmanageable, these plagues were found only in small corners of our otherwise sparkling cities and their impressive cultural monuments. But now that we canot apply any effective force against violent tent campers with access to an ativist judge, the protection of our Homeland's heritatage has fallen into uncertain hands.

XI:
The I-I Gap and The Magna Carta's Failure

The *Magna Carta* has long been celebrated as the cornerstone of modern democracy. Even though this medieval reconcilliation between King John and a smallish number of his rebellious Barons covered only a small segment of England's aristocracy, it was forever afterward assumed to grant full rights to all free men in England.

After King John affixed his signature on many Latin copies of this Great Charter, he distributed them to the rebelious Barons who had cornered him on Runnymede Meadow on June 15, 1215. Of the 63 detailed provisions of this cherished Charter, the excerpts that have stood the test of time are two proclamations. The first is from Aricle 52:

> To any man whom we have deprived or dispossessed of lands, castles, liberties, or rights, without the lawful judgment of his equals, we will at once restore these [abrogated] rights.

And the second is this confirmatory proclamation from Article 63:

A Hidden Cause of Widespread Homelessness

> It is accordingly our wish and command that the English Church shall be free, and that men in our kingdom shall have and keep all these liberterties, rights and concessions, well and peaceably in their fullness and entirety for them [i.e., the Barons] and their heirs, of us and our heirs, in all things and all places forever.

This commitment to remove liberties and rights from the whimsical commands of kings and submit them to the "lawful judgment of equals" was indeed an advance in England's govenance. Because King John had been widely hated for his abusive laws and empty promises, these new proclamations were accepted with more gratitude than expected.

Even though nobody at that time could foresee that the *Magna Carta* provided the foundation of the West's progress toward democratic self-governance, it did in fact play an important role in the development of democracy in Europe and especially in the new nations of the Western Hemisphere, where individual freedom dependended on democratic government.

For example, Alexander Hamilton, in his Federalist 84, commented on Article 39 of the *Magna Carta*, which stated that "No man shall be seized or imprisoned ... except by ... the law of the land." Hamilton realized that a autocratic king could be as whimsical and arbitrary as King Geeorge III, but the law of a just land should be orderly and consistently applied.

In Hamlilton's mind, the *Magna Carta* provided the foundation for the later English idea of *Habeas Corpus* (Latin for "Show me the Body"), that is, before an alleged criminal could be arrested and imprisoned, evidence must first be presented to a magistrate that shows that the accused had likely broken the law. Under this umbrella, unjustified imprisonment could be rightfully prevented.

Of course, thick-skulled King John was not sufficiently clear-minded to remember what he had signed, nor did he have the capacity to understand the consequences of breaking his word, which he and his 25 Barons managed to do on multiple occasions, leading to civil war. Thus Pope Innocent III soon annulled the *Magna Carta*, because it specifically violated the Divine Right of Kings, on which the Universal Church depeneded for the enforcement of Catholic dogma. Supposedly, a righteous Catholic monarch would reliably rebuff a multitude of heresies, which the Barons of Runnymede were likely to embrace if their dangerous freedom were not annulled.

Despite the blemished setting of Runymeede in 1215, the Founders of the United States self-consciosly drew on both the *Magna Carta* and the Ten Commandments to guarantee that justice be enforced under the rule of law and not dictated by unpredictable monrchs, be they religious or secular. Thus, those who met in Philadelphia in 1789 appended to their Constitution a Bill of Rights, precisely ten in number, like the Ten Commandments.

However, despite the positive cultural power of both the *Magna Carta* and the American Bill of Rights, the buried animosities in Runnymede have now sprung back to life, nurtured by the despair of those who believe that they have been unreasonably thrust into, or even below, the I-I Gap. Suddenly, many of our fellow citizens are certain that they have been deceived about America's promises. Without knowing an iota about King John and his *Magna Carta*, or about King George III and George Washington, or about Abraham Lincoln's risking his own life, his soldiers' blood, and his nation's treasure to end the evil of slavery, our disapointed citizens nonetheless believe that they have been robbed of what they are owed.

In response to this imagined injustice, statues of America's foremost heroes are now being torn down, without any benefit accruing to the thuggish topplers. What matters now is not justice and liberty but punishing the American liars who suffer an inborn racism and a brutish intolerance of folk whose unusual beliefs are scorned rather than enshrined under the U.S. Constitution's guarantee of freedom of thought, behavior, and speech.

And since many of these excluded groups have been unjustly herded into or even below the I-I Gap, they are naturally driven to bellicose protestations, even if they achieve nothing but a worsening of their lot. Thus the formerly celebrated Christopher Columbus, who was seeking a more efficient trade route to India by sailing westward from Europe, has now been accused of pursuing a mission to import African slaves to America while exterminating the American Indians who were already there.

Though Columbus had likely heard doubtful myths about a Western Continent rich in gold, when he arrived in the Caribbean Islands in the 1490's he reasonably believed he that he had indeed found a true westward route to India. And so he named these islands the West Indies.

Of course, he could not foresee that he was opening an escape route from the constant internecine wars of autocratic Old Europe into a brave new world, where the better parts of European civilization might be nurtured. Columbus himself inadvertently demonstrated how the European urge to learn, to explore, and to invent had liberated Europeans from lives that were, as Hobbes would describe 150 years later in his *Leviathan*, "solitary, poor, nasty, brutish, and short."

And so, on October 12, 1792, the 300th anniversary of Columbus's epic landing in the New World, the now infamous Tammany Hall in New York City declared a holiday. Though many thought that the graft-ridden Tammany Hall was an unsuitable sponsor of a holiday honoring the man who had given a second chance to Europe's stumbling civilization (Italy itself did not consolidate its waring Duchies and Papal States until 1869), it was not until 1968 that President Lyndon Johnson signed the legislation that made Columbus Day an official holiday in the United States, where Columbus's name had already been bestowed on the capital cities of Ohio and South Carolina, and an unofficial Holliday was already being celebrated everywhere in the United States, including my kindergarten.

Thus the U.S. joined other nations in Western Hemisphere, including Colombia, where the very name of the Nation honors both the man and the principles that his celebratory day represents: *el Día de la Diversidad Étnica y Cultural de la Nación Colombiana* (the Day of Ethnic and Cultural Diversity of the Colombian Nation).

But Columbus's contribution to the ideals of liberty and exploratory ingenuity of the United States is now of little interest to those who find themselves unfairly confined to the I-I Gap. Thus, angry rioters toppled a statue of Columbus and hauled it away from Saint Paul, Minnesota's capital:

A Hidden Cause of Widespread Homelessness

Nor are Columbus's contributions to liberty in Latin America of any current interest to those demonstrators who toppled a statue of that nation's namesake in Barranquilla, Colombia, on June 28, 2021:

Also occurring in our new age of revised history, bizarre theories of America's racist foundation have arisen in academia to replace our supposedly ill-conceived choice of heroes. For example, we now have before us the celebrated "1619 Project," whose purpose is to shoehorn the entire history of the United States into a procrustean bed of delusional reasoning. Robert C. Thornett, in his essay for *Quillette,* "Forgetting vs. Overcoming: Abuses of History and the 1619 Project," carefully documents the mendacity of the project's publisher, *The New York Times*, and its creator, Nikole Hannah-Jones, who claims that the United States was founded on the virtue of slavery:

> In the Hulu docuseries, the 1619 Project's founder Nikole Hannah-Jones states that the project's goal is to "reframe the country's history by placing the consequences of slavery and the contribution of black Americans at the very center of our national narrative."… In theory it was a worthy goal. But in practice … The "one thing" to which it [the 1619 Project] tries to reduce American history is a unidimensional struggle between white oppression and black victimhood … from 1619 to today.

I cite Thornett's critique of the *1619 Project* to remind Ms. Hannah-Jones that the American Colony of Rhode Island had already outlawed slavery before America's Revolutionary War against England, that we have made much progress in interracial relationships since our brutal Civil War to emancipate former slaves, that in 1619 no American Colony yet existed, and that of those that were later founded none would have for decades a port that could accommodate the triangular slave trade from Europe to West Africa and from thence to the Caribbean and South America, and then home to England, Spain, or Portugal.

I also want to suggest to Ms. Hannah-Jones that it is not America's invented founding on the institution of slavery that has provoked our current troubles; rather, it is our growing I-I Gap that is forcing more and more uprooted Americans to conclude that their hopes to obtain the American rewards of Life, Liberty, and the Pursuit of Happiness are being unfairly smothered by nefarious hands. And since nefarious hands are invisible and cannot be indited, Ms. Hannah-Jones and other activists must now seek a more visible, or at lease more legible culprit, such as the founding history of the United States, which can be revised when necessary.

Yes, since the late Sixteenth and early Seventeenth centuries, Spanish, Portuguese, and English privateers purchased slaves in the markets of West Africa and then sold their human cargo in South America and the Caribbean. And by the early Nineteenth century there were indeed large slave markets in the Southern States of the US, most notably in New Orleans, where the remnants of its old slave market can still be visited. But slavery was never the founding principal of any nation in the Western Hemisphere.

The United States was founded on the English principles of liberty, as formulated by John Locke and John Stuart Mill. In South America, Simon Bolivar rejected slavery and was known as the Liberator of the former Spanish Colonies of Panama, Colombia, Peru, Ecuador, Bolivia, and Venezuela. And Brazil's "Liberator," Pedro I, was also a known abolitionist who was proud to have been born on Columbus Day in 1798.

And then, in the long-established United States. Abraham Lincoln, a dark horse Republican candidate, won the 1860 presidential election largely on the basis of his earlier rejection of slavery as an assault against the human dignity of every American citizen, black or white.

When Stephen A. Douglas, Lincoln's opponent in the Illinois Senatorial debates of 1858, used his renowned oratorical skills to echo the strong pro-slavery passions that were then being bellowed in Congress and across the land, Lincoln had to tiptoe around his belief that the Negro's moral and intellectual incapacities appeared unequal to those of the White man only because the enslaved Negro was deliberately kept uneducated.

Beset by Douglas's critical attention to his every word, Lincoln had to proceed carefully as he spoke during the debate in Quincy, Illinois:

> ... There is no reason in the world why the negro is not entitled to all the rights enumerated in the Declaration of Independence—the right of life, liberty, and the pursuit of happiness. I hold that he [the Negro] is as much entitled to these as the white man. I agree with Judge Douglas that he [the Negro] is not my equal in many respects, certainly not in color—perhaps not intellectual and moral endowments; but in the right to eat bread without the leave of anybody else which his own hand earns, he is the equal of Judge Douglas, and the equal of every other man.

Since Lincoln was self-educated by reading the fundamental texts of Western Civilization by candlelight, he was slyly able to assign Douglas to the same "equal" class that included a Black slave and "every other man." In this way, Lincoln clarified that illiteracy was not fundamental to the nature of the enslaved Black Man, nor was slavery fundamental to the mores of the United States of America. The principles of the signers of the *Declaration of Independence* constituted the true foundations of our civilization. This was so despite whatever Judge Douglas had to say to the contrary. All human beings, Black, White, or otherwise, were entitled to liberty and an educated life.

Nevertheless, now that so many of out fellow citizens are wallowing in or below the I-I Gap, there have suddenly arisen thugs who topple and deface statues of Abraham Lincoln, such as the one felled during the riots in Portland, and the one spraypainted in London's Parliament Square, where a squad was summoned to repair the damage:

Those who vandalized these statues believed that the undeservedly honored 16th President of the United States was just another liar who had promised more than he could deliver. And in this worldview, history can be re-made to justify a new revolt against an old betrayal.

When did this fictional betrayal begin? In 1619, or possibly 1617, or 1620, depending on whom one relies for the original story, privateers carried some two hundred slaves on a British ship named the *White Lion* with the intention of marketing them to sugarcane plantations in Bermuda. After offloading all but 20-30 slaves, the privateers headed back to England, from whence they could repeat their triangular slave route. However, during a roaring storm, the *White Lion* was blown far off course to the haven of Point Comfort (now the location of Fort Monroe in Hampton, Virginia).

The marooned privateers and their few unsold salves, says Ms. Hannah Jones, clearly enacted the founding principle of what would become, some 150 years later, the United States of America.

A Hidden Cause of Widespread Homelessness

Because everything that Lincoln ever said or did no longer mattered, Ms. Hannah-Jones was able to tell her readers that the voyage of the *White Lion* represented the plan to initiate and perpetuate American slavery.

That the *White Lion*'s "Founding event" was simply an accident of bad weather could not be considered by the creators of *The 1619 Project*, for a second slave ship, called the *Treasurer*, was also blown westward by the same storm and landed in Virginia a few days after the *White Lion*. It, too, carried a few unsaleable slaves. This second event, according to the scholarly pushers of *The 1619 Project*, irrefutably proved that both the *White Lion* and the *Treasurer* were in the business of using Black slaves to found White America.

That the obvious purpose of these privateers was to increase their own treasure could not be considered by the meticulous historians of *The 1619 Project*, who blinded themselves to the likelihood that the windblown slave traders of 1619, or thereabouts, had no thought in their storm-tossed minds of founding a nation dedicated to slavery or to anything else in the haphazard harbor of Point Comfort.

These slavers lacked both the motive and the manpower to establish a Colony of *any* kind. Without food or the means to purchase it, they bartered for supplies by surrendering their few slaves, who may have wound up in Jamestown, which was founded in 1620, or maybe they were freed, according to other, disputed sources.

Now, why would the *New York Times*, this longstanding newspaper of record, endorse this questionable story, and why would the intelligent creators of *The 1619 Project* ignore the doubtfulness of their interpretation of the storm-driven voyages of the *White Lion* and the *Treasurer*? Were these privateers really far more important to the fate of the United States than the voyages of the *Nina*, *Pinta*, and *Santa Maria, The Mayflower,* or the naval battle between the Union's *Monitor* and the Confederate *Merrimac*?

Might the creators of *The 1619 Project* be so resentful of the imagined White terror that has forced many of their fellow citizens either into or below the I-I Gap, that they overblew the importance of the *White Lion* while ignoring the origin of slavery in Africa?

Queen Nzinga, born in 1583, ruled a large empire in Sub-Saharan and West Africa, where she ordered her armies to transport captive slaves from the interior to markets on the coast of what is now called Angola. She is said to have provided nearly 200,000 slaves to the Portuguese during the very era of the 1619 privateers. The savvy and powerful Queen committed herself to provide this huge quantity of slaves in order to obtain an alliance that would help secure her empire and *its* colonies.

The Portuguese engraving, taken from Getty Images and shown below, was designed in about 1626 and carries this caption:

> During the[ir] long Wars Of Invasion, The Portuguese Met A Formidable Adversary in Queen Nzinga of Matamba.

The engraving, shows the royally guarded Queen sitting on the back of a handy slave while negotiating with two Portuguese ambassadors:

A Hidden Cause of Widespread Homelessness

During their long wars of invasion, the Portuguese met a formidable adversary in Queen Nzinga of Matamba

The creators of *The 1619 Project* likely knew of Queen Nzinga, for she was active in the international slave trade during the era on which our scholars focused their expertise. But our scholars did not bother mentioning this "Formidable Adversary," for she offered no support to *Project*'s far-fetched claim that white privateers on a ship named the *White Lion* had sailed specifically to Virginia in order to establish Black Slavery as the foundation stone of the nation that would be declared some 150 years later.

The 1619 Project's re-imagined founding of the United States is so bizarre that it requires a broader understanding of what we mean by homelessness. How one construes the history of the United State reflects how at home one feels in the nation whose Declaration of Independence was signed not in 1619 but in 1776, and whose Constitution was signed in 1787. Those who *do* feel at home in the nation founded on these old documents call themselves "Patriots," and those who feel betrayed by these same documents express contempt for the misplaced pride of their bigoted country.

Thus we find ourselves living in a country where ungovernable colonies of tent campers who are supported by those who also feel homeless in the larger sense of being betrayed by the very heroes who supposedly founded a nation that has promised equality for all but has delivered nothing but threats to those who object to the restrictive rules of bigoted elitists.

Of course not everyone in an encampment feels homeless in the larger sense of being betrayed by America, and neither do *all* the campers' virtuous supporters. But many of those encamped in parks, and even some domiciled in relatively safe communities, *do* feel less at home in a nation that has found no effective solution to the ever-enlarging I-I Gap. And thus we are thrust back into the necessity of creating a life-enhancing way to cut this most challenging of Gordian Knots. Are Americans at home in America, or are they homeless in the imaginary United States of 1619?

And similar questions have arisen in many other civilized nations.

XII:
Homelessness is Now an International Plague

As homeless encampments spread stealthily throughout the United States, an even more troubling phenomenon has been creeping into many other Western Nations. As is the case at the US's unprotected southern border, unidentifiable and unvetted migrants are now slipping into other Western nations.

Some of the local inhabitants of these recently overwhelmed nations recognize these uninvited seekers as a threat to their homeland's longstanding values and customs, while others in the same homeland are more deeply motivated by compassion. And some have more radical motivations, like those creators of *The 1619 Project*, who hope that better-informed voters will overcome those who refuse to recognize the nefarious foundation of their homeland's perverse values, which are not as admirable as elementary students are misleadingly instructed.

In this muddied context, we learn of the perspective of Hungary's Prime Minister, Victor Orbán, as reported by Reuters on July 28, 2022:

Hungarian Prime Minister Viktor Orban stuck to his anti-immigration stance on Thursday but insisted it was not rooted in racism after his recent remarks that Hungarians did not want to become "peoples of mixed race" drew fire at home and abroad.

Orban has spoken about maintaining "ethnic homogeneity" in Hungary before, taking a hard line on immigration since 2015. But his comments in Romania on Saturday, when he said that in contrast to Western Europe's "mixed-race world" where people mixed with arriving non-Europeans, Hungary was not a mixed-race country –- hit a nerve, drawing condemnation from the United States, the European Union, Jewish groups, and academics.

[To which, Orban responded] "I am the only politician in the EU who stands openly for an anti-immigrant policy," Orban told a joint news briefing with Austrian Chancellor Karl Nehammer in Vienna. "This is not a race issue with us, this is a cultural issue," he said. "It happens sometimes that I say something in a way that can be misunderstood but … the position I stand for is a cultural, civilization stance."

…

Earlier this week, European Commission vice president Frans Timmermans said on Twitter "poisonous" racism had no place in Europe that drew its strength from diversity.

But Budapest's chief rabbi Zoltan Radnoti told Reuters any communication "talking about races, pure races, and mixing of races" was unacceptable.
…
The head of the Association of Hungarian Jewish communities, Slomo Koves, though, while critical of Orban's language, said he did not believe his speech was racist. "He portrayed a certain, very legitimate conservative view on European and World politics," he said. Concerns about the retreating Western civilization or unchecked mass illegal immigration from the Middle East were part of it, he said.

Thus, homelessness is no longer a merely local issue of self-contained skid roads, and not even a single nation's issue of lost self-confidence, but a worldwide worry about whether one should actually defend the imagined civilization that supposedly constitutes the bedrock of ones irreplaceable homeland. Currently, the news on this issue concerns the vicious wars about the legitimacy about The Ukraine's Homeland, Putin's Russian Empire, and the equally vicious war regarding the legitimacy of the Jews' right to their ancient Homeland versus the counterclaims of Hamas and Hezbollah .

If Ukrainians and their unique culture have no legitimate rights to The Ukraine, then a brute like Putin might easily justify his claim that those rights belong to the Russian Empire, for many of those who reside in Eastern Ukraine speak Russian. But if that is the essential criterion for establishing borders, then it should follow that Russia should return much of Eastern Russia to the Chinese, who were forced to cede much of their vast territory after a series of invasions by Tsarist armies.

Below is a map of the Tsar's enlarged Russian Empire, with the tan-colored area marking lands that Russia usurped from China in 1858, and the rose-colored area identifying territory that the Tsarists acquired after imposing the Treaty of Peking on the hapless Chinese in 1860:

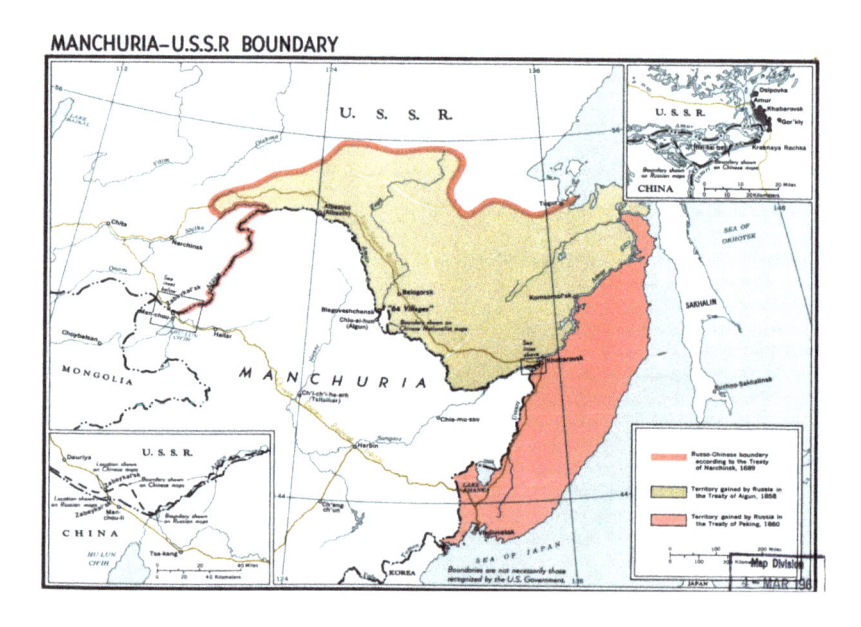

At the bottom tip of the rose-colored area sits the modern Russian city of Vladivostok, 90% of whose residents are native Russian speakers. This is so because over the last 160 years, the Tsarists and then the Soviets expelled many longtime Chinese residents. And most educated Russians know that Russian power didn't make much headway across the Ural Mountains into Siberia and Northern China until the reign of Tsar Ivan the Terrible late in the Sixteen century, comparatively late when compared to the ancient Chinese presence in Northeastern Asia.

And there are still many Chinese who remain in the vast, under-populated regions of far-eastern Russia, and these are being joined by many new Chinese speakers, who are now slipping across the long northern border between China and Russian. For these hard-working descendants from an old agrarian civilization are *not* thriving in China's new, industrialized, and smog-choked megacities.

As the residents of Russian Vladivostok look across the Sea of Japan into China and consider China's growing population, which reached 1.4 billion in 2022, they must wonder how long they can feel at home in a nation that possesses the earth's largest land mass but whose population has shrunk from 170 million in 1940 to a 144 million in 2023, just one tenth of China's teeming billions, many of whom recall their old homes in eastern Siberia.

Russia simply has insufficient population to defend much of her homeland, a problem common to almost all advanced countries around the world that are failing to replace their aging populations. This requires women of reproductive age to produce on average 2.1 children. Some nation's reproduction rate is so low that soon they will be unable to care for their elderly. For example, prosperous South Korea now faces a dwindling future with a replacement rate of about 0.72.

Russia suffers even graver threats to their homeland. Below is a map of the population densities in Russia's various hinterlands:

Victor M. Erlich, PhD, MD

Population Density of Russia

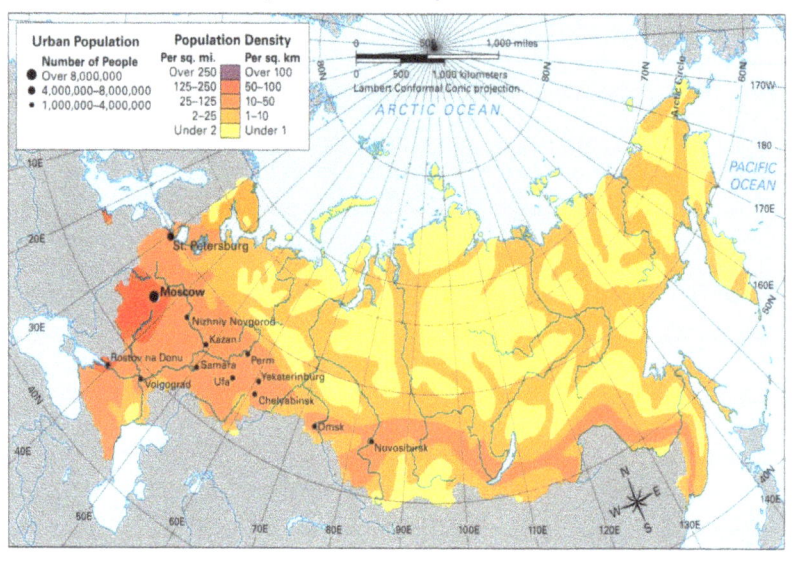

The small red and persimmon areas on the map represent urban centers and their surroundings, where Russian is spoken, and the population does its best to maintain the civilization of Tolstoy and Pushkin. In the light orange regions of Greater Russia, fewer than 10 souls per square kilometer defend Russia against any intruders who might wish to follow those who once invaded Old Rus until Peter the Great put an end to the invasive Finns and Mongols. And in the yellow areas there is hardly a single soul per square kilometer to defend Catherine the Great's Empire and its French-speaking aristocracy, or Stalin's Workman's Paradise, or Putin's megalomaniacal fantasy of actualizing the dreams of both Catherine and Stalin.

In any case, few citizens anywhere in the modern world are eager to follow the fatal decisions of Julius Caesar and Catherine the Great to seek an ever-enlarging empire. As has been the case for millennia, most people seek to feel at home with fellow citizens, a satisfaction that can never be achieved by stealing it from a people that already has it, such as the Ukrainians on the western border of desperate Russia, or modern Jews huddling on the borders of both Levantine chaos and Western decadence in Europe and the U.S.

So there we are. Too many of us are either locally homeless in encampments, or nationally homeless under the leadership of liars and deceivers like Abraham Lincoln, or losers in the international race to obtain dignity in the glorious realms above the I-I Gap.

Like all scarce commodities, the satisfaction of feeling deeply at home is often prohibitively expensive to acquire if not already possessed. Despite its huge land mass and even larger population, China finds it necessary to send its intelligent students to universities in the West to steal proprietary secrets, and even to steal more homeland by implanting pseudo-islands in international waterways, like the South China Sea. The Russian Federation suddenly removes Crimea on the Black Sea from The Ukraine, which, in Russia's view, enjoys undeserved pride in its fruitful homeland, called the breadbasket of Eastern Europe.

Additionally, Putin, a modern Tsar, bombs Ukrainian maternity wards and kidnaps large numbers of Ukrainian children in order to beef up the falling Russian population while simultaneously winnowing Ukrainian reproduction. But this brutal strategy has accomplished nothing but push both Russians and Ukrainians deeper into discontent about the current state of their homelands.

In our age of readily available metrics, we can now measure a nation's satisfaction with life in their homeland. Even though the metrics of a nation's happiness are not verifiably objective, they do tell us that nations composed by an amalgam of incompatible tribes, such as The Russian Federation and Mao's revolutionary conglomeration, are less happy, less creative, and feel less at home than do the citizens of smaller nations who share common values.

The *2024 World Happiness Report*, compiled by Gallup and other research organizations, used a range of variables to rank a large number of nations according to the extent of their happiness. The variables included GDP per-capita, social support, freedom to make personal choices, standards of living, health, generosity of the population, perception of corruption, and life expectancy. Those in the happiest top ten are mainly in Northern Europe, where most residents are content with the work-habits and generosity of their fellow citizens :

1. Finland (for the fourth year in a row)
2. Denmark
3. Iceland (despite volcanic eruptions)
4. Sweden
5. Israel (despite war and mayhem)
6. Netherlands
7. Norway
8. Luxembourg
9. Switzerland
10. Australia

In this survey, most respondents did not care that citizens in Finland and Holland felt happier than those in Iran, Afghanistan, and Zimbabwe. What mattered most to citizens everywhere was whether or not their homeland had a small but noisy faction, homegrown or imported, that felt unjustly homeless in their otherwise thriving homeland, be it in Sweden, England, The Ukraine, or the United States, which does not rank in the top ten. Even if a nation is relatively content as a whole, a small cabal of angry activists can set a nation like the U.S. back on its heels.

This is often true of citizens in the U.S. and elsewhere in the West, where a sufficient number feel unjustly outcast from their preferred homeland by unjust usurpers, such as Christopher Columbus and Abraham Lincoln in the United States, and Margaret Thatcher of England, and Victor Orbán of Hungary, and even Israel's Benjamin Netanyahu, against whose rightwing policies thousands have rioted daily.

But the most powerful and widespread rejection of ones homeland arises in those who feel unjustly deprived of any valuable skill after having devoted their so-called higher education to their university's politically correct curricula, which dooms them to a place in or below the I-I Gap.

Again and again one hears young adults all through the industrialized West complaining that they will never be able to purchase a home despite having obtained a degree from a famous university. For in an age of constant innovation, happiness and a home in which to display ones gold-embossed diploma is exclusively reserved for those who possess sufficient ingenuity to master up-to-date skills in science, technology, engineering, or mathematics. Those forlorn souls without these advanced skills will not obtain a mortgage, no matter how low rates may go.

In many North-European centers of satisfied achievers, and on the campuses of many esteemed U.S. universities, smallish coteries of activists are naturally angry when they realize that by majoring in gender studies, or Mongolian art, or interracial politics, they have unjustly made themselves useless castoffs, bereft of the skills necessary to thrive in an innovated world.

Having gained little from venting their wrath on Christopher Columbus and Abraham Lincoln, many of our uprooted neo-Luddites turn their resentment on tiny Israel, a nation that must have nefariously gained its high rank among the successfully happy by oppressing the innocent, hardworking, Palestinian strivers, who have expended enormous energy not on establishing an admirable civilization on their land but on building some 500 kilometers of underground tunnels stocked with armaments and rockets, which to this day are still being fired at the loathsome colonist, Israel, whose people have never colonized any land other than their own.

Many Gazan sympathizers hope to evade their own fears of being marooned in a homeless enclave by unthinkingly supporting the destruction of Israel, the one successful Homeland that is currently enjoying the fruits of a literate, lawful, and creative civilization. For Israel's creative response to innovation has inevitably provoked the resentment of those who feel unjustly thrust into or below the I-I Gap, where the excluded do not accept their lack of ingenuity lightly, even if their enclave is as large as Russia.

Thus those who feel bereft of a decent homeland are *not* eager to join those who support the Ukrainians in their existential war against the Russian invaders of *their* Homeland. Many liberal Americans would rather see their money spent at home on those who have been betrayed by their own homeland's misbegotten values.

This troubling development raises the question of what might be done to encourage disaffected American citizens to re-evaluate their having abandoned all attachments to their homeland, which was founded on the values of life, liberty, and the socially responsible pursuit of happiness. Thus the effort to revitalize our commitment to our homeland is no easy task, for our current, often violent, disagreements are in many ways more unbridgeable than those that produced the horrendous bilateral slaughter of the American Civil War.

Though the opposing armies of the American Civil War shared a common conviction that "life," "liberty," and "the responsible pursuit of happiness" must be preserved, their conflicting understandings of these ethical terms allowed them to slaughter each other for four years. But because the Union's and the Confederacy's mutual slaughter arose from clashing interpretations of the same principles, they shared enough common ground to allow the Confederacy's General Robert E. Lee to surrender peacefully to the Union's commanding General Ulysses S. Grant at Appomattox Court House on April 9, 1865.

The opposing Generals and their officers were formally attired (Lee apparently said, "I expect to be taken as a prisoner, so I should dress appropriately for the occasion."), one side in blue, the other in grey, with neither side lording it over the other. Both sides respectfully held their hats in hand. For both believed that they had honorably defended justice, as they understood it.

So immediately after the signing ceremony, Lee and Grant shook hands, as on this celebratory postcard, based on a painting by Thomas Nast:

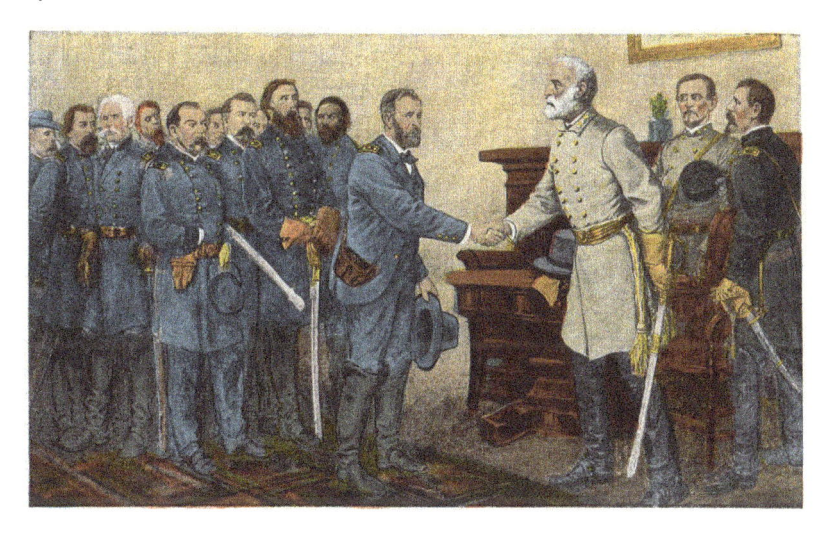

This almost convivial event still stands in marked contrast with the nastiness that accompanied the Treaty of Versailles to end World War I and the begrudged surrenders of Germany and Japan to end World War II. With the American custom of pursuing life and liberty persisting in the background, Grant and Lee sincerely sought peace, despite the fact that the civil war took the lives of more than 600,000 soldiers. The Confederacy lost about 30 percent of military-eligible men, and both armies commonly destroyed homes, entire towns, livestock, and farmland, which led to more than a million civilian deaths from disease and starvation.

Nevertheless, General Lee did not wallow in resentment or resistance. Instead he did everything he could to restore peace and harmony. This led to a hearing in the U.S. Congress on May 28, 1924, during which a bill was passed to restore Lee's former home, Arlington House, in recognition of the Confederate General's contribution to the healing of the nation's wounds from its self-destructive Civil War.

According to Douglas Southall Freeman's *R.E Lee: A Biography*, published in four volumes in 1935, Lee should be considered a national hero:

> The Confederates came to consider it as much the course of patriotism to emulate General Lee in peace as it had been to follow him in war. More than any other American, General Lee kept the tragedy of the war from becoming a continuing calamity.

Even Elizabeth Bowen Pryor, who was not one of Lee's respectful historians, praised Lee's commitment to peace, as demonstrated by:

> [The] enlightened position he took to foster peace and rebuild the South in the early aftermath of the war. This was his grand visionary moment ... His courageous military restraint in 1865 and his early words of reconciliation were more than a face-saving final bow from the stage. They offered a model for a great and proud army that felt itself humiliated, a salve for a devastated citizenry, a running start towards reconciliation. Some may be disappointed that Lee was not perfectly noble in every word and deed during the postwar period. Yet [his] tremendous forbearance under pressure of prosecution [for treason], ... and personal ostracism is noble.

Ms. Pryor's praise of Robert E. Lee recalls Lincoln's conciliatory words in his Second Inaugural Address on March 4, 1865:

> With malice toward none; with charity for all; with firmness in the right, let us strive on to finish the work we are in; to bind up the nations wounds ...

And, indeed, Lee's surrender quickly led President Lincoln to sign the much-anticipated Emancipation Proclamation.

Though it took many long years for the U.S to make any significant strides toward racial harmony, few citizens ever gave up entirely on Lee's and Lincoln's belief that the loss of blood and treasure on the road to Appomattox was to be both regretted and accepted as necessary in a nation that was compelled to fulfill its dedication to equal justice for all.

But today, in the midst of our current disdain for the unfulfilled hopes of Lee and Lincoln, we have lost confidence in both of these humane leaders who were trapped in a Greek tragedy, in which our current activists tear down statues of both, with intense animus focused on the statue that had been erected in honor of the humane General Robert E. Lee, who made the error of following mankind's fatal propensity to overestimate the value of oneself and ones tribe. And so tragic General Lee, nicknamed "The Marble Man," has recently been reduced, like Macbeth, to a noisy tale "told by an idiot," as his dismembered statue was carted off from his marble monument in Richmond Virginia, the final Confederate Capital:

A Hidden Cause of Widespread Homelessness

A nation cleared of both heroes and villains, all of whose particular beliefs and acts have been erased, is unlikely to serve as a model of a self-sustaining homeland for anybody.

Do we or do we not value living in a national homeland that represents tested values that can withstand malice of every kind?

XIII:
How Might a Treasured Homeland Be Recreated?

To explore the possibility of restoring confidence in the U.S. as a homeland honored for its valued principles, let us consider another national monument, the one dedicated to an African American, Dr. George Washington Carver (1864-1943). A worthy biography of Dr. Carver was provided in 2001 by Janet and Geoff Benge in the Heroes of History series: *George Washington Carver: From Slave to Scientist*, now in its eighth printing.

Because nobody bothered to record the birthdates of slaves or the names of their fathers, and because George's father, Giles, died in an accident before his yet-unborn son arrived, the clever young boy was content to work without knowing the date of his birth or his proper last name. Circumstances made it proper for him to use his former owner's last name, for Moses Carver proudly supported his adopted son as he voraciously pursed his education.

Because of his accomplishments, Dr. Carter became a famous scientist, educator, humanitarian, and artist. But recently he is more often ignored than celebrated, despite deriving more than 300 valued products from peanuts (including milk, paint, medicinal oils, cosmetics, and ink), and more than 100 products from sweet potatoes (including synthetic rubber and postage-stamp glue that can be safely licked).

Carver even developed an early form of gasoline, which so impressed Henry Ford that in 1942 the carmaker presented the acclaimed inventor a fully stocked laboratory so that he could continue his internationally recognized research:

A Hidden Cause of Widespread Homelessness

    And, for his many contributions to American prosperity, Dr. Carter was honored by having his portrait and microscope embossed on U.S. postage:

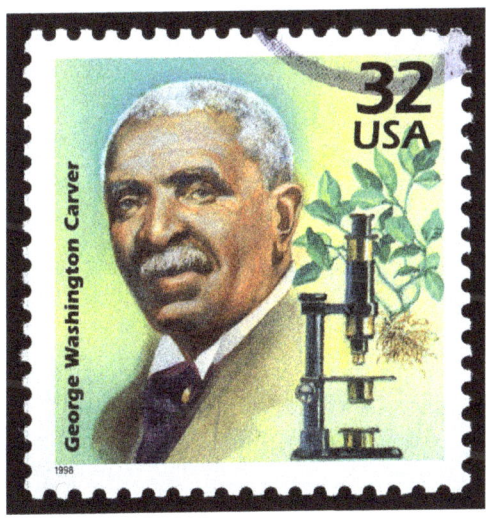

And after Dr. Carter died, President Franklyn Roosevelt signed authorization to build the George Washington Carver National Monument in Diamond, Missouri, on the site where the impressive man was born a slave just before the end of the Civil War. This National Monument features 210 well-cultivated acres, the Moses Carver House, and a stately bust of Doctor George Washington Carver.

Early in his journey to this honor, the ambitious student studied piano and art at Simpson College in Indianola, Iowa, where his talented painting of botanical subjects so impressed his teachers that they encouraged him to study botany at Iowa State University in Ames, Iowa. After graduation, he worked tirelessly to improve the agricultural capacities of America's struggling farmers, including his fellow African Americans.

And with his training in music and art, our innovative scientist was also driven by a lifelong commitment to painting. Here is a photograph of his adding finishing touches to his last known painting, entitled "The Yucca," a plant whose diverse scientific and esthetic qualities he had studied carefully:

A Hidden Cause of Widespread Homelessness

With a creative and innovative model like George Washington Carver in our minds, we might recreate a homeland in which citizens are confident that they will overcome the trauma of our most recent Civil War, the one between those who soar above the Innovation-Ingenuity Gap and those who have not yet managed to do so. And with that accomplished, we might yet again call the fruitful Land of the United States of America our home.